USELESS INFO

A Curious Compilation of Weird and Witty Facts

Vernon Knight

CONTENTS

INTRODUCTION

Welcome to "Useless Info: A Curious Compilation of Weird and Witty Facts" by Vernon Knight. Within these pages, you are about to embark on a delightful journey into the world of the bizarre, the amusing, and the utterly unexpected. In a world filled with information overload, these tidbits of knowledge may seem frivolous, but they hold a unique charm that transcends their "uselessness."

This book is a treasure trove of peculiar and entertaining facts, carefully curated to bring a smile to your face and pique your curiosity. From the animal kingdom's quirkiest behaviors to the whimsical laws that govern countries, from the fascinating inventions that changed our lives to the humorous myths that have shaped cultures, and from the intricacies of the human body to the eccentricities of historical figures—every page is brimming with the strange and the comical.

Our journey begins with the animal kingdom, where you'll discover creatures with peculiar habits and characteristics that often rival the wildest of human imagination. From the depths of the oceans to the heights of the skies, animals of all shapes and sizes have their moments of oddity.

Next, we delve into the realm of human invention, where genius and eccentricity often walk hand in hand. Learn about bizarre contraptions, offbeat discoveries, and inventions that, while sometimes laughable, have forever altered our world.

From there, we travel across the globe, exploring the quirkiest and most perplexing laws ever enacted by governments, all on the continent of Europe, Asia, Australia, and Africa. Some laws seem like they belong in the annals of absurdity, while others reveal surprising cultural nuances.

But our journey doesn't stop there. We venture into the fascinating world of history, uncovering the strange, humorous, and often unbelievable tales of historical figures, their peculiar habits, and the myths that have woven themselves into the fabric of their stories.

The voyage continues with a comprehensive exploration of the human body, highlighting its idiosyncrasies and marvels. Our bodies are a constant source of amazement, from the mysteries of the brain to the quirks of our senses.

And finally, we dive into the world of pop culture, where cartoons, books, movies, and music have left their indelible mark. Discover the hidden secrets, humorous anecdotes, and bizarre coincidences that make these cultural phenomena even more fascinating.

As you turn the pages of "Useless Info," prepare to be entertained, surprised, and occasionally astounded by the wealth of weird and witty facts presented here. These nuggets of information may not change the course of history or solve the mysteries of the universe, but they will undoubtedly bring a smile to your face and remind you that curiosity and laughter are among the greatest gifts of being human.

So, without further ado, let's embark on this delightful journey through the delightful and eccentric world of "Useless Info." Enjoy the ride!

ANIMALS

Sloths only poop once a week and make a dangerous journey to the ground to do so.

A group of flamingos is called a "flamboyance."

Male seahorses give birth and can carry up to 2,000 babies at once.

A snail can sleep for three years straight.

The star-nosed mole has the fastest eating speed of any mammal, taking only 230 milliseconds to identify and consume food.

The tongue of a blue whale can weigh as much as an elephant.

The echidna, a spiky anteater, lays eggs, but it's a mammal.

When a group of crows gathers, it's known as a "murder" of crows.

Some owls have asymmetrical ear placements, allowing them to hear in 3D and pinpoint the exact location of their prey.

The male ferret will often die within a few months if it doesn't find a mate because of a hormone imbalance.

A group of pugs is called a "grumble."

The tardigrade, or water bear, can survive extreme conditions, including the vacuum of space and boiling temperatures.

Octopuses have three hearts: two pump blood to the gills, and one pumps it to the rest of the body.

The male seagull proposes to a female by giving her a tasty piece of food. If she accepts, they become a couple.

Capybaras, the world's largest rodents, are known for forming unlikely friendships with other animals, such as cats, birds, and monkeys.

Platypuses lay eggs and produce milk, making them one of the few mammals that can make their own custard.

The pistol shrimp can snap its claw so quickly that it creates a shockwave and bubbles that reach temperatures hotter than the surface of the sun.

The electric eel can produce shocks of electricity strong enough to stun its prey or deter predators.

The tongue of a giraffe is so long that it can clean its ears with it.

Kangaroos cannot walk backward, thanks to their unique leg and hip structure.

The mimic octopus can imitate the appearance and behavior of various marine creatures, including lionfish, flatfish, and sea snakes.

Goats have rectangular pupils, which allow them to see almost 360 degrees around them.

The honeybee can recognize human faces and remember them for a long time.

A group of hedgehogs is called a "prickle."

The tongue of a hummingbird can flap at an incredible rate, up to 80 times per second.

Some species of frogs can freeze during the winter and thaw out in the spring.

The Aye-Aye, a type of lemur, uses its long middle finger to tap on trees and extract insects to eat.

Penguins have a gland above their eyes that filters salt from their bloodstream, helping them survive in salty seawater.

The narwhal, often referred to as the "unicorn of the sea," has a long spiral tusk that can grow up to 10 feet long.

The male firefly emits light signals to attract a mate, and different species of fireflies have distinct flash patterns.

The African elephant is the largest land animal and can weigh as much as 14,000 pounds.

Axolotls are known for their regenerative abilities and can regrow lost body parts, including limbs and even parts of their brain.

The male seahorse is the one responsible for carrying and birthing the babies, sometimes up to 2,000 at a time.

The mantis shrimp has the most complex eyes in the animal kingdom, capable of seeing polarized light and a vast range of colors.

Cows have best friends and can become stressed when separated from them.

Female hyenas have a pseudo-penis that is almost indistinguishable from the male's genitalia.

A group of rhinoceroses is called a "crash."

The Brazilian horned frog has a unique method of swallowing prey: it flips its entire body inside out.

The male ferret can die from prolonged sexual frustration.

Pufferfish inflate themselves to deter predators and can become almost spherical in shape.

Some ants keep "herds" of aphids as a source of honeydew, a sweet substance they produce.

The naked mole rat is immune to cancer and doesn't experience pain from certain irritants.

When hippos are upset, they often defecate and spin their tails like a helicopter to spread their feces.

The green basilisk lizard is known as the "Jesus Christ lizard" because it can run on water for short distances.

The tapeworm has the longest known body length of any parasite, reaching up to 82 feet in some cases.

The manatee's closest living relative is the elephant.

Some species of ants can carry objects up to 50 times their body weight.

The naked mole rat is cold-blooded and can survive without oxygen for an extended period.

Cuttlefish can change their skin color and texture to blend in with their surroundings or communicate with other cuttlefish.

Male seagulls propose to females by offering them a shell or a piece of food. If the female accepts, they become mates.

The tongue of a woodpecker wraps around its skull to protect its brain from the force of pecking.

The quokka, known as the "world's happiest animal," often appears to be smiling due to its upturned mouth.

The aardvark's name comes from the South African Afrikaans language and means "earth pig," although it's not related to pigs.

The axolotl remains in its larval form throughout its life, never undergoing full metamorphosis into an adult amphibian.

The lyrebird is a master of mimicry, imitating various sounds it hears in its environment, including chainsaws and camera shutters.

The kakapo parrot is one of the heaviest parrot species and is known for its clumsiness and inability to fly.

The poison dart frog's skin secretes toxic chemicals that indigenous people use to poison the tips of blow darts.

The pink fairy armadillo is the smallest species of armadillo and is rarely seen due to its nocturnal and burrowing habits.

The hagfish, often referred to as a "slime eel," produces copious amounts of slime when threatened, making it hard for predators to grab.

The male frigatebird inflates a large red pouch on its throat to attract females during mating displays.

A group of jellyfish is called a "smack."

The barnacle has the longest penis relative to its body size in the animal kingdom, up to 50 times its body length.

The platypus has electroreceptors in its bill that help it detect the electrical signals of prey underwater.

The vampire bat has specialized heat sensors on its nose to locate blood vessels in its prey's skin.

When hippos yawn, they are not necessarily tired but are

displaying their large teeth as a sign of aggression or warning.

The binturong, also known as the "bearcat," smells like buttered popcorn due to a scent gland on its tail.

Male narwhals may engage in "sword fights" with their tusks during disputes over territory or mates.

A group of raccoons is called a "nursery."

The axolotl can regenerate not only limbs but also spinal cord and heart tissue.

The golden poison dart frog's skin holds enough poison to kill 10 adult humans.

The banded iron formation in the Pilbara region of Western Australia contains fossils of some of the earliest life forms on Earth, including stromatolites created by ancient cyanobacteria.

The blue-footed booby gets its name from its vibrant blue feet, which it uses in courtship displays.

The blobfish, often considered one of the world's ugliest animals, appears quite different in its natural deep-sea habitat than in photos taken at the surface.

The geoduck clam has one of the longest lifespans of any animal, with some individuals living up to 100 years or more.

The lyre-tailed nightjar, a bird found in Central and South America, has tail feathers that resemble lyres and are used in elaborate courtship displays.

The Surinam toad carries its eggs on its back, where they eventually hatch into fully formed tadpoles.

The proboscis monkey has a large, pendulous nose that amplifies vocalizations and is considered attractive to potential mates.

The quokka is known for its friendly and photogenic expression, often referred to as the "world's happiest animal."

The secretary bird, despite its name, is actually a bird of prey and not an office worker.

The tufted deer has fangs rather than antlers, which it uses in territorial disputes and to impress mates.

The axolotl has the unique ability to regenerate not just limbs but also its spinal cord, heart, and other organs.

The male ferret can die from a hormone imbalance if it doesn't find a mate.

The star-nosed mole has 22 fleshy appendages on its snout that are incredibly sensitive and allow it to identify and consume prey rapidly.

The mudskipper, a fish that can breathe air and crawl on land, uses its pectoral fins to move around on mudflats.

The pangolin is often called a "walking pinecone" due to its armored scales, which are made of keratin, the same substance as human fingernails.

Some species of ants "farm" aphids, protecting them and harvesting the sweet honeydew they produce.

The male binturong, or bearcat, has a scent gland on its tail that smells like buttered popcorn.

The tongue of a chameleon can extend to more than twice its body length, allowing it to catch insects from a distance.

The tapeworm can grow to astonishing lengths, with some specimens reaching up to 82 feet.

The narwhal, known as the "unicorn of the sea," has a long spiral tusk that can grow up to 10 feet in length.

The electric eel can produce shocks of electricity to stun prey or deter predators.

Sloths only defecate once a week and make a dangerous journey to the ground to do so.

The male bowerbird creates intricate and artistic "bowers" adorned with colorful objects to attract females. Each species has its unique style.

A group of owls is called a "parliament."

The lyre-tailed nightjar, a bird found in Central and South America, has tail feathers that resemble lyres and are

A group of dolphins is called a pod.

A group of kangaroos is called a mob.

A group of monkeys is called a troop.

A group of penguins is called a colony.

A group of whales is called a pod.

The hyena is the only mammal that laughs.

The honey badger is known for its fearless and aggressive behavior.

The honey badger is immune to the venom of most snakes.

The wombat can poop cubes.

The male anglerfish is the smallest fish in the world, and it attaches itself to the female anglerfish, which is much larger, and lives off of her body.

The vampire squid is a deep-sea creature that has bioluminescent tentacles that it uses to attract prey.

The komodo dragon is the largest lizard in the world, and it can grow up to 10 feet long.

The Komodo dragon can run up to 18 miles per hour, which is faster than most humans.

DINOSAURS

The word "dinosaur" means "terrible lizard," but not all dinosaurs were large or lizard-like.

Dinosaurs lived on Earth for over 165 million years, while humans have been around for just a fraction of that time.

Birds are considered living dinosaurs because they evolved from small, feathered theropods.

The largest dinosaur known is Argentinosaurus, estimated to be up to 100 feet long and weighing up to 100 tons.

The smallest dinosaur was the size of a chicken, like the microraptor.

Some dinosaurs, like the Stegosaurus, had brains the size of a walnut.

The Tyrannosaurus rex had one of the largest brains among the dinosaurs.

The Brachiosaurus, a sauropod dinosaur, had a longer neck than any other known dinosaur.

The longest dinosaur name is "Micropachycephalosaurus" (24

letters).

The shortest dinosaur name is "Eoraptor" (7 letters).

The Velociraptors in the "Jurassic Park" movies were depicted much larger than their actual size.

Stegosaurus had plates on its back but didn't use them for defense; their purpose is still debated.

Some dinosaurs had feathers for insulation, display, or both.

The "Duck-billed" dinosaurs, like Parasaurolophus, had crests on their heads, possibly for vocalization.

The Ankylosaurus had a bony club at the end of its tail that it could swing like a weapon.

The Triceratops had three facial horns and a large frill at the back of its head.

The Spinosaurus had a sail-like structure on its back, possibly for temperature regulation.

The first dinosaur fossil discovered and scientifically described was Megalosaurus in 1824.

Some dinosaurs were herbivores, while others were carnivores, and some were omnivores.

The fastest dinosaur was the cheetah-like Dromiceiomimus, capable of running up to 60 mph.

Some herbivorous dinosaurs had complex digestive systems, similar to modern cows, to break down tough plant material.

Many dinosaurs had sharp teeth, but some were adapted for crushing plants or grinding food.

Apatosaurus was originally named "Brontosaurus" but later reclassified.

The "Iguanodon" was one of the first dinosaurs to be discovered and named.

Some dinosaurs, like the Oviraptor, were mistakenly thought to be egg thieves because they were found near eggs.

The name "Pterosaur" means "winged lizard," but they were not dinosaurs; they were flying reptiles.

Pterosaurs came in various sizes, from small as a sparrow to larger than a giraffe.

The Pteranodon had a wingspan of up to 30 feet.

The largest pterosaur, Quetzalcoatlus, had a wingspan of up to 36 feet.

Some dinosaurs, like the Dcinonychus, had sickle-shaped claws on their feet for hunting.

The Allosaurus was one of the top predators of the Jurassic period.

The Allosaurus had serrated teeth designed for cutting through flesh.

The Spinosaurus was likely the largest carnivorous dinosaur and may have been semi-aquatic.

The Stegosaurus had a brain that weighed less than 3 ounces.

The Carnotaurus had tiny arms compared to its body size.

The "Mother of all Lizards," the Komodo dragon, is related to ancient dinosaurs.

The first dinosaur eggs were discovered in Mongolia in the 1920s.

The Brachiosaurus was once thought to be the heaviest dinosaur, but Argentinosaurus surpassed it in size.

Many dinosaurs were social creatures and lived in herds, like modern-day buffalo.

The longest dinosaur eggs ever discovered are from the Hypselosaurus, reaching up to 19 inches in length.

Some dinosaurs, like the Allosaurus, had a cannibalistic nature, as indicated by fossil evidence.

The Microraptor was a small, feathered dinosaur capable of gliding.

The Velociraptor had a sickle-shaped claw on each foot that it used for hunting.

The Maiasaura was a dinosaur known for taking care of its young, as indicated by fossilized nesting grounds.

The largest Tyrannosaurus rex skull measures over 5 feet long.

The first dinosaur to be cloned in the "Jurassic Park" series was a Velociraptor.

The Spinosaurus was a likely contender for the apex predator of its time, even larger than T. rex.

Some dinosaurs, like the Therizinosaurus, had incredibly long claws, possibly for self-defense or gathering food.

The Iguanodon was one of the first dinosaurs to be assigned a species name.

The Brachiosaurus may have been capable of rearing up on its hind legs to reach high foliage.

The Brontosaurus never truly existed as a separate species but was based on a misidentified Apatosaurus.

The first dinosaur footprints were discovered in England in 1825.

Some dinosaurs, like the Triceratops, had hundreds of teeth during their lifetime.

The Psittacosaurus, a small herbivorous dinosaur, had a beak similar to a parrot.

The largest dinosaur eggs belonged to the Titanosaur and could be over a foot long.

Some dinosaurs, like the Archaeopteryx, are considered transitional forms between dinosaurs and birds.

The Anomalocaris, a marine creature from the Cambrian period, is often mistaken for a dinosaur but predates them by millions of years.

The Giganotosaurus was one of the largest theropod dinosaurs and lived in what is now Argentina.

The Brachiosaurus is estimated to have had a heart weighing over 1,000 pounds to pump blood to its head.

The Diplodocus, a long-necked dinosaur, had nostrils on top of its head, which allowed it to breathe while its body was submerged in water.

The first nearly complete dinosaur skeleton ever found was the Hadrosaurus foulkii in 1858.

The Ankylosaurus had armor plating on its body and a club-like tail for defense.

The first recorded dinosaur fossil find in North America was a dinosaur tooth discovered in 1854.

The Triceratops was not the only ceratopsian dinosaur; there were many other species with different horn and frill configurations.

The Megalodon, a prehistoric shark, coexisted with some dinosaurs and had teeth over 7 inches long.

The Sauroposeidon was the tallest dinosaur, with a neck that could reach over 40 feet in length.

The first identified dinosaur to be named was the Megalosaurus in 1824.

The Dilophosaurus had a frill around its neck that it could flare up to scare away predators.

The most intelligent dinosaur was the Troodon, which had a brain the size of a chimpanzee's.

LAWS

Austria: It's illegal to mow your lawn on Sundays.

Austria:You can't name your child anything that is not on an approved list.

Belgium: You can't wash your car in your driveway.

Bulgaria: It's illegal to wear camouflage clothing in public.

Croatia: Nudity is allowed at beaches, but only if it's in designated areas.

Cyprus: You can be fined for wearing flip-flops or high heels while driving.

Czech Republic: It's illegal to feed pigeons in public squares.

Denmark: You must check under your car for sleeping children before starting it.

Estonia: It's illegal to drive a dirty car.

Finland: Taxi drivers must pay royalties if they play music in their cars.

France: You must carry a breathalyzer in your car, but not using it can result in a fine.

Germany: It's illegal to run out of fuel on the Autobahn.

Greece: High-heeled shoes are banned at ancient monuments.

Hungary: You can't whistle in a public place at night.

Iceland: It's illegal to have a dog in the capital city, Reykjavik.

Ireland: You can't be drunk in a pub.

Italy: It's illegal to sit on the steps of a monument or eat near one in Florence.

Latvia: You can't wear revealing clothing in public places.

Lithuania: You must smile at all times in public, except at funerals or visiting the sick.

Luxembourg: It's illegal to name your child anything other than what's on the approved list.

Malta: You can't be shirtless or in swimwear outside of the beach area.

Netherlands: It's illegal to pee in canals in Amsterdam.

Norway: You must have your headlights on at all times, even during the day.

Poland: Winnie the Pooh is banned from public playgrounds for not wearing pants.

Portugal: You can't pee in the ocean.

Romania: It's illegal to swear in public.

Russia: You can't drive a dirty car.

Serbia: It's illegal to have a dirty car.

Slovakia: It's illegal to name your child something that doesn't appear on the approved list.

Slovenia: It's illegal to wash your car in front of your house.

Spain: You can be fined for wearing flip-flops while driving.

Sweden: It's illegal to paint your house without a government permit.

Switzerland: You can't own just one guinea pig because they get lonely.

United Kingdom: It's illegal to die in the Houses of Parliament.

United Kingdom: It's illegal to handle a salmon suspiciously.

United Kingdom: It's illegal to enter the Houses of Parliament wearing a suit of armor.

Albania: It's illegal to enter a public building wearing a mask or hood.

Andorra: It's illegal to not be a member of a local shooting club.

Bosnia and Herzegovina: You must register your guests with the local police within 24 hours.

Macedonia: It's illegal to be drunk in public.

Montenegro: It's illegal to drive a dirty car.

San Marino: You can't walk a dog on a leash longer than 2 meters.

Ukraine: You can't wear a hat indoors.

Belarus: It's illegal to applaud in public places.

Estonia: You can be fined for not wearing a reflector at night.

Latvia: You must carry a first aid kit in your car at all times.

Lithuania: You can be fined for not smiling in public.

Moldova: You must carry a fire extinguisher in your car.

Azerbaijan: It's illegal to chew gum in public.

Georgia: It's illegal to smoke in outdoor public spaces.

Kazakhstan: It's illegal to take photos of police officers or government buildings.

Kyrgyzstan: You can't play the accordion in public places.

Tajikistan: It's illegal to name your child anything that doesn't appear on the approved list.

Turkmenistan: It's illegal to have a black car.

Uzbekistan: You can't use a satellite dish without government permission.

Vatican City: It's illegal to walk a dog in St. Peter's Square.

Albania: It's illegal to wear military clothing in public.

Andorra: It's illegal to perform the national anthem in a comedic or satirical manner.

Bosnia and Herzegovina: You can't wear high heels or stilettos while driving.

Macedonia: It's illegal to name your child anything that doesn't appear on the approved list.

Montenegro: It's illegal to name your child anything that doesn't appear on the approved list.

San Marino: It's illegal to name your child anything that doesn't appear on the approved list.

Ukraine: You can't name your child anything that doesn't appear on the approved list.

Belarus: It's illegal to name your child anything that doesn't appear on the approved list.

Armenia: It's illegal to name your child anything that doesn't appear on the approved list.

Azerbaijan: It's illegal to name your child anything that doesn't appear on the approved list.

Georgia: You can be fined for not smiling in public.

Kazakhstan: It's illegal to wear a bikini in public parks.

Kyrgyzstan: You can be fined for not smiling in public.

Tajikistan: It's illegal to name your child anything that doesn't appear on the approved list.

Turkmenistan: You can be fined for not smiling in public.

Uzbekistan: It's illegal to name your child anything that doesn't appear on the approved list.

Afghanistan: It's illegal to fly kites in Kabul.

Bahrain: It's illegal to have a dirty car.

Bangladesh: It's illegal to play loud music during prayer times.

Cambodia: It's illegal to honk your horn near a pagoda.

China: You must visit your aging parents often, as not doing so is illegal.

India: It's illegal to dance near the Taj Mahal.

Israel: It's illegal to bring bears to the beach.

Laos: It's illegal to step on money, which features images of the king.

Lebanon: It's illegal to honk your horn in the city.

Maldives: It's illegal to import idols for religious worship.

Mongolia: You must not whistle indoors, as it's considered bad luck.

Myanmar: It's illegal to leave the country with any Buddha images.

Nepal: It's illegal to kill a cow, as they are considered sacred.

Pakistan: It's illegal to carry more than two kilograms of potatoes.

Philippines: It's illegal to not sing the national anthem with enthusiasm.

Australian Capital Territory: It's illegal to fly a kite or play games in public places that annoy or disrupt others.

Australian Capital Territory: It's against the law to swim in Lake Burley Griffin unless authorized.

Australian Capital Territory: You can't keep a pet rabbit or hare in the capital.

New South Wales: It's illegal to disrupt a wedding or funeral.

New South Wales: You can't be in possession of 50 kilograms or more of potatoes in one place at one time.

New South Wales: You can't release more than 99 balloons in a 24-hour period.

Northern Territory: It's illegal to participate in or promote a public brawl.

Northern Territory:You can't handle fish in suspicious circumstances.

Queensland: It's illegal to possess a laser pointer without a reasonable excuse.

Queensland: It's against the law to possess a skateboard in certain public places.

Tasmania: You can't ride a bike without a bell.

Tasmania: It's illegal to annoy wildlife, including penguins, whales, and seagulls.

Queensland: It's illegal to engage in swordplay in public.

Tasmania: It's against the law to drive a white vehicle on Sundays and public holidays unless you're a farmer.

Victoria: It's illegal to wear pink hot pants after midday on a Sunday.

New South Wales: It's illegal to release more than 99 balloons in a 24-hour period.

Burundi: You can't play drums after 10:00 PM.

Congo (Brazzaville): You can't wear a tracksuit in public.

Congo (Kinshasa): It's illegal to play music with lyrics in a bar or restaurant.

Kenya: It's illegal to be in possession of a plastic bag.

INVENTIONS

The Slinky was originally designed as a spring to stabilize sensitive naval equipment, but it became a popular toy by accident when it tipped over and started "walking" down a shelf.

The first computer mouse was made of wood and had two wheels, not the optical or laser sensors we use today.

The earliest form of the alarm clock was called the "knocker-upper," and it involved paying someone to tap on your window with a long stick to wake you up.

The invention of the bicycle paved the way for the development of the modern automobile. In fact, some early cars were referred to as "horseless carriages."

Thomas Edison, the inventor of the light bulb, was afraid of the dark.

The slotted spoon was invented by Samuel W. Francis, who was frustrated with the messy job of fishing tea leaves out of his tea.

The Frisbee was originally a pie tin from the Frisbie Pie Company, and college students in the 1940s began tossing them around for fun.

The first message sent over the internet was "LO," which was meant to be "LOGIN," but the system crashed after the first two letters.

The Post-it Note was invented by Spencer Silver, who was trying to create a super-strong adhesive but ended up with a weak one that could be easily removed.

The world's first speeding ticket was issued in 1902 when a New York City taxi driver was caught driving 12 miles per hour.

The modern fire hydrant was invented by Frederick Graff in 1801, and it hasn't changed much in design since then.

The invention of the microwave oven was accidental. Percy Spencer, an engineer working with radar technology during World War II, noticed that a chocolate bar in his pocket melted while he was standing near a magnetron (a microwave tube).

The potato chip was invented in 1853 by George Crum, a chef who sliced potatoes thinly and fried them in response to a customer's complaint that the fries were too thick.

The idea for the Super Soaker water gun came to inventor Lonnie Johnson while he was working on a heat pump using water as a coolant.

The first known use of the smiley face emoticon :-) was in 1982 by computer scientist Scott Fahlman.

The windshield wiper was invented by Mary Anderson in 1903 after she observed a trolley car driver struggling to see through a snowstorm.

The first TV remote control was called the "Lazy Bones," and it was connected to the television with a long cable.

The inventor of the Segway, Dean Kamen, once claimed that his invention would be as significant as the internet. Despite its practical uses, it didn't quite reach that level of impact.

Velcro was inspired by burdock burrs that stuck to the inventor's dog's fur during a hike.

The earliest form of a selfie stick was created in the 1980s by a Japanese inventor named Hiroshi Ueda.

The concept of the "Pet Rock" as a novelty item became a cultural phenomenon in the 1970s. People purchased ordinary rocks as pets, complete with instruction manuals.

The first recorded use of the term "robot" was in a 1920 play by Czech playwright Karel Čapek called "R.U.R. (Rossum's Universal Robots)."

The world's first vending machine, created in the early 1st century AD, dispensed holy water in Egyptian temples when a coin was inserted.

The concept of the "Doomsday Clock," which symbolizes the countdown to global catastrophe, was created in 1947 by the Bulletin of the Atomic Scientists.

The idea for the first disposable diaper came to Marion Donovan, a mother, when she used a shower curtain as a diaper cover.

The famous Nobel Prize-winning physicist Albert Einstein

invented a refrigerator that didn't require electricity. It used ammonia, but it never gained popularity.

The game of "Trivial Pursuit" was created by two Canadian journalists who wanted to invent a game to make money so they could play more Scrabble.

The first known documented "selfie" was taken in 1839 by Robert Cornelius, a pioneer in photography. He had to stand still for 15 minutes to capture the image.

The invention of the wheel is considered one of humanity's greatest innovations, yet no one knows who actually invented it, as it dates back thousands of years.

The Popsicle was invented by an 11-year-old boy named Frank Epperson, who accidentally left a glass of soda with a stirring stick outside in freezing temperatures.

The inventor of the Frisbee, Walter Frederick Morrison, was cremated, and his ashes were molded into a Frisbee after his death.

The concept of the modern bicycle was created in the 19th century by Karl Drais, but it was initially called the "Draisine" or "running machine."

The Post-it Note was initially deemed a failure when it was first developed by 3M because it wasn't strong enough adhesive. It only became a hit when someone found a creative use for it.

The invention of the first practical telephone is attributed to Alexander Graham Bell, but his rival Elisha Gray filed a patent for a similar device on the same day. Bell got the patent because he arrived at the patent office first.

The concept of the flushing toilet was invented by John Harington in the late 16th century. He installed one for Queen Elizabeth I but didn't gain much recognition for it.

The invention of the electric toaster was a game-changer for breakfast. Before that, people toasted bread over an open flame.

The "Mousetrap" board game was invented by a British man named Leslie Scott, who was inspired by stacking wooden blocks in a coffee shop.

The concept of the bar code was inspired by Morse code. The first barcode was used on a pack of chewing gum in the early 1970s.

The original patent for the fire hydrant was lost in a fire, leading to disputes over its invention.

The "Slinky" was originally designed to be used as springs in sensitive instruments aboard naval ships.

The invention of the disposable razor is credited to King Camp Gillette, who believed that creating a product people would throw away would lead to recurring sales.

The concept of the roll-on deodorant was inspired by a ballpoint pen.

The microwave oven was discovered when Percy Spencer, an engineer, noticed a candy bar in his pocket had melted while working with a magnetron.

The concept of the Post-it Note adhesive was developed accidentally when Dr. Spencer Silver at 3M was trying to create a super-strong adhesive.

The concept of the shopping cart was introduced in 1937 by Sylvan Goldman, a grocery store owner, who wanted customers to buy more groceries.

The "Slinky" was accidentally created when Richard James, a naval engineer, knocked over a spring and saw how it "walked" down the stairs.

The first electric toothbrush was invented in Switzerland in 1954, but it took a while for it to gain popularity.

The invention of the modern condom can be traced back to the 19th century when they were made from animal intestines.

The concept of the pacemaker was inspired by a chance discovery by engineer Wilson Greatbatch, who was working on an oscillator for heart rhythm research.

The invention of the inkjet printer was inspired by the "coffee ring effect," where spilled coffee dries in a ring shape due to capillary action.

The concept of the Super Soaker water gun, created by engineer Lonnie Johnson, was inspired by his work on high-pressure water systems for NASA spacecraft.

The invention of the snow globe can be traced back to a surgeon named Erwin Perzy, who created the first one in 1900 while trying to develop a brighter light source for surgical lamps.

The invention of the Etch A Sketch was inspired by an invention intended for military use. André Cassagnes, a French electrician, created a joystick-controlled device to help draw diagrams for engineers.

The concept of the modern fire extinguisher was developed by British Captain George William Manby in 1813. It was initially designed to extinguish fires on naval ships.

The idea for the disposable camera, known as the "Fujifilm QuickSnap," came from a Fujifilm executive's frustration with not being able to take photos of his child's school sports day.

The iconic Swiss Army Knife was originally created for soldiers but became popular with civilians after World War II. It includes various tools such as a knife, screwdriver, and even a toothpick.

The concept of the wind-up radio was developed by Trevor Baylis, a British inventor, as a way to provide information to people in remote areas without access to electricity.

The concept of the "Dyson Ball" vacuum cleaner, known for its maneuverability, was inspired by a wheelbarrow wheel that could move in any direction.

HISTORICAL PLACES

The Leaning Tower of Pisa, Italy began leaning during construction due to unstable soil, and it leans at an angle of about 3.97 degrees.

Stonehenge was built over 4,000 years ago, but no one knows for sure why it was built or how the massive stones were transported.

Contrary to the belief that the Great Wall of China is visible from space, it's often too narrow to be seen without the aid of telescopic lenses.

Llamas and alpacas are used to help maintain the grass at Machu Picchu by grazing, reducing the need for lawn mowers.

The Taj Mahal changes color with the time of day. It appears pinkish in the morning, white in the day, and golden in the moonlight.

Ancient Romans used a type of retractable awning called a "velarium" to provide shade to spectators of the Colosseum.

The Eiffel Tower can be 15 cm taller during the summer months due to the expansion of its iron structure in the heat.

The sculptor of Mount Rushmore, Gutzon Borglum, originally

intended to carve the figures from head to waist, but funding ran out.

The Great Pyramid in Egypt was the tallest man-made structure in the world for over 3,800 years.

The Statue of Liberty's full name is "Liberty Enlightening the World," and it was a gift from the people of France to the United States.

Some of the columns of the Parthenon in Greece are slightly tilted to create the illusion of straight lines due to the curvature of the temple.

The Moai statues were transported across the island using a system of ropes, sleds, and manpower.

The Alhambra in Spain has a room called the "Hall of Abencerrages," which is known for its ceiling that is said to resemble the night sky. Legend has it that the room was the site of a mass execution.

The nose of the Sphinx of Giza is missing, and its exact removal is still a mystery. Some theories suggest it was shot off by Napoleon's troops.

The Acropolis museum in Athens was designed to have the same dimensions as the Parthenon to display its sculptures as they were originally placed.

The Tower of London has been used for various purposes, including a royal palace, a prison, and a treasury. It's also home to a group of ravens with a superstition that they must be kept there to protect the kingdom.

The Roman Baths in Bath, England, were built around 70 AD, and people still bathe in the natural hot spring waters today.

The Angel of the North, a massive sculpture, has a wingspan wider than a Boeing 767.

On the spring and autumn equinoxes, the sunlight casts a shadow on the steps of the El Castillo pyramid, in Chichen Itza, Mexico, creating an illusion of a snake descending.

Vatican City is the smallest independent state in the world, both in terms of area and population.

The Alamo in Texas was originally a mission and is famous for the Battle of the Alamo during the Texas Revolution.

The Palace of Westminster has over 1,000 rooms, 100 staircases, and 3.2 kilometers of corridors.

During the construction of Christ the Redeemer Statue, Brazil, workers used a small chapel at the top of the mountain as a workshop and office space.

Petra is famous for its rock-cut architecture, including the iconic Treasury building featured in "Indiana Jones and the Last Crusade."

The ancient city of Teotihuacan contains the Pyramid of the Sun and the Pyramid of the Moon, aligned with celestial bodies.

The Brandenburg Gate in Berlin was once used to symbolize the division between East and West Berlin during the Cold War.

While one of the Seven Wonders of the Ancient World, there is still debate among historians about whether the Hanging Gardens of Babylontruly existed.

The Pantheon in Rome has a hole in the roof called the "oculus," which allows rain to enter but drains through the floor.

The One O'Clock Gun at Edinburgh Castle is fired every day (except Sundays) at precisely 1:00 PM, a tradition dating back to 1861.

Kissing the Blarney Stone at Blarney Castle is believed to bestow the gift of eloquence, but it requires leaning backward over a parapet to reach.

The Palace of the Popes in Avignon, France, was home to seven consecutive popes during the 14th century, during a period of papal schism.

The Great Buddha was originally housed in a temple, but a tsunami in the 15th century washed the temple away, leaving the statue exposed to the elements.

There is a statue of St. John of Nepomuk on the Charles Bridge in Prague. Rubbing it is believed to bring good luck and ensure your return to Prague.

The Palace of Knossos on the island of Crete is considered Europe's oldest city, dating back to around 2,000 BC.

The Nazca Lines, in Peru, a series of enormous geoglyphs in the Nazca Desert, can only be fully appreciated from the air.

The Tower Bridge in London is often mistaken for London Bridge, but they are two distinct structures.

The Mount of Beatitudes overlooking the Sea of Galilee is traditionally believed to be where Jesus delivered the Sermon on the Mount.

The Palace of Fine Arts in San Francisco was originally constructed for the 1915 Panama-Pacific Exposition and was intended to be a temporary structure.

The Giant's Causeway, in Northern Ireland, is famous for its hexagonal basalt columns, and legend has it that it was built by a giant named Finn McCool.

The Mont Saint-Michel, an island commune in Normandy, has an unusual phenomenon where the tide can rise quickly and turn the island into a temporary peninsula.

The Tower of Hercules in A Coruña, Spain, is the oldest Roman lighthouse still in use today, dating back to the 2nd century AD.

The Terracotta Army, created to protect the tomb of China's first emperor, Qin Shi Huang, consists of thousands of life-sized statues.

The Banaue Rice Terraces, in the Philippines, are often referred to as the "Eighth Wonder of the World" and were carved into the mountains over 2,000 years ago.

MYTHOLOGY

Norse Mythology (Scandinavia): Thor once dressed as a bride to retrieve his stolen hammer, Mjölnir.

Greek Mythology: Pygmalion fell in love with a statue he had carved, and Aphrodite brought it to life as his wife, Galatea.

Japanese Mythology: The mythical creature Tengu is believed to have a long, red nose capable of extending to ridiculous lengths.

Hawaiian Mythology: Pele, the goddess of volcanoes, is said to create new land by urinating lava onto the earth.

Aztec Mythology (Mexico): The Aztecs believed that the sun was created from the severed head of a god, and it required daily sacrifices to keep it moving across the sky.

Chinese Mythology: There's a myth about a man named Wu Gang who was punished by the Moon Goddess to endlessly chop down a self-healing cassia tree on the moon.

African Mythology: The Yoruba people believe that the god Obatala created humans out of clay but got drunk and made some of them imperfect.

Native American Mythology (Lakota Sioux): The trickster figure,

Iktomi, is known for his silly antics, like turning sticks into snakes to scare people.

Roman Mythology: In the myth of Romulus and Remus, the twins were raised by a she-wolf before founding the city of Rome.

Polynesian Mythology: The hero Maui tried to slow down the sun by lassoing it with a rope to make the days longer.

Egyptian Mythology: In one version of the creation myth, the world was created from the tears of the god Atum.

Inuit Mythology: Sedna, the sea goddess, is said to have long, tangled hair that becomes sea creatures when she combs it.

Baltic Mythology: The Latvian god of thunder, Perkons, was believed to be a thundering giant with a huge beard.

Hindu Mythology: In the story of the churning of the ocean, the gods and demons used a mountain as a churning stick and a giant snake as a rope.

Mayan Mythology (Central America): The Maya believed that humans were created from maize dough by the gods.

Finnish Mythology: In the Kalevala, a famous epic, a character tries to build a boat from the fragments of an enormous beer barrel.

Celtic Mythology: In Irish folklore, leprechauns are mischievous fairies who hide their pots of gold at the end of rainbows.

Aboriginal Mythology (Australia): The Rainbow Serpent is a

creation being believed to have shaped the landscape and left winding rivers in its wake.

Slavic Mythology: The firebird is a mythical creature known for stealing golden apples and leaving behind a trail of fiery feathers.

Mesoamerican Mythology (Aztec): The god Xolotl, who is associated with death and lightning, was believed to have the head of a dog.

Native American Mythology (Hopi): In the Hopi creation myth, the Earth was created by a playful god, Spider Grandmother.

Roman Mythology: The god Priapus was known for his oversized, permanent erection, which was considered a symbol of fertility.

Inca Mythology (Peru): The Inca believed that they were the descendants of the sun, and their emperors were called "Children of the Sun."

Maori Mythology (New Zealand): According to legend, the hero Maui once tried to slow down the sun by trapping it in ropes, causing the days to be longer.

Japanese Mythology: The myth of the "Hare of Inaba" tells the story of a hare who tricks sharks into forming a bridge.

Polynesian Mythology: In Hawaiian mythology, Kamapua'a, a half-man, half-pig deity, was known for his shape-shifting abilities.

Chinese Mythology: The goddess Nuwa is said to have created humans by molding them out of yellow clay, much like pottery.

Native American Mythology (Navajo): The trickster figure Coyote is known for his silly and often disastrous adventures.

Sumerian Mythology (Mesopotamia): The goddess Inanna descended to the underworld but had to be bailed out by other gods after being trapped there.

Greek Mythology: In the story of the Trojan War, Achilles' mother dipped him in the River Styx to make him invulnerable, but she held him by his heel, leaving it unprotected.

African Mythology (Yoruba): The god Eshu is a trickster figure who plays pranks on people and the other gods.

Russian Mythology: The Domovoi is a household spirit believed to protect the home but can also be mischievous if not appeased.

Hawaiian Mythology: The goddess Pele is said to travel in the form of a white dog, and it's considered bad luck to see her.

Inuit Mythology: Sedna, the sea goddess, is said to have had her fingers chopped off by her father, creating sea creatures in the process.

Norse Mythology: The god Loki once transformed into a mare and gave birth to an eight-legged horse named Sleipnir.

Hindu Mythology: The god Ganesha has the head of an elephant and is often depicted riding a mouse.

Roman Mythology: The goddess Venus is said to have been born from the sea foam, which is why she's often depicted rising from the ocean.

Mayan Mythology (Central America): The Maya believed that the earth was flat and supported by a giant crocodile.

Korean Mythology: In Korean folklore, there is a creature called the "gumiho" or "nine-tailed fox" that can transform into a beautiful woman to seduce men.

Scottish Folklore: The Loch Ness Monster, known as "Nessie," is said to inhabit Loch Ness in Scotland, and there have been numerous sightings of this elusive creature.

Japanese Mythology: In Japanese folklore, the "kappa" is a mischievous water creature that loves cucumbers and is known for challenging humans to sumo wrestling matches.

African Mythology (Zulu): According to Zulu mythology, Unkulunkulu, the creator god, vomited the people, animals, and plants onto Earth.

Roman Mythology: The god Janus is depicted with two faces, one looking forward and one looking backward, symbolizing his role as the god of beginnings and transitions.

OUR BODY

Goosebumps: When you experience strong emotions or get cold, tiny muscles called arrector pili contract, causing your hair to stand on end, creating goosebumps—a vestige of our evolutionary ancestors' responses to cold or threats.

Nose and tongue Print: Similar to fingerprints, every person has a unique nose and a unique tongue print, making them potential forms of identification.

Skin Shedding: The skin is the body's largest organ, and it sheds millions of dead skin cells every day, making up a significant portion of household dust. Over your lifetime, you'll shed about 40 pounds (18 kilograms) of skin.

Saliva Production: Over a lifetime, the average person produces enough saliva to fill two swimming pools.

Fingerprints: Your fingerprints are not only unique but also highly durable. Even if you burn your fingertips, your fingerprints will regenerate.

Blushing: Blushing is controlled by your autonomic nervous system and can also occur on the lining of your stomach.

Hiccups: Hiccups are caused by sudden, involuntary contractions of the diaphragm muscle. Even fetuses experience hiccups in the womb.

Sneezing Speed: Sneezes can travel at speeds of up to 100 miles per hour (161 kilometers per hour).

Blinking: On average, you blink about 15-20 times per minute, adding up to approximately 28,800 blinks per day.

Hair Growth: Human hair grows at a rate of about 0.5 inches (1.25 centimeters) per month.

Farting: The average person passes gas about 14 times a day.

Smelling Capacity: Humans can distinguish between around 1 trillion different odors.

Taste Buds: You have about 10,000 taste buds on your tongue, and they are replaced every 10 to 14 days.

Heartbeat: Your heart beats around 100,000 times a day and pumps about 2,000 gallons (7,500 liters) of blood daily.

Loud Stomach: The sounds your stomach makes when it's hungry or digesting food are called borborygmi.

Earwax Production: Earwax is produced to protect your ears, but excessive earwax can cause temporary hearing loss.

Yawning: Yawning is contagious and can even be triggered by reading or talking about yawning.

Belly Button Bacteria: The average belly button is home to over 2,000 different species of bacteria.

Blinking Coordination: When you blink, your brain temporarily shuts off, so you don't see the world go dark every time you blink.

Mucus Production: Your body produces about 1 to 1.5 quarts (1 to 1.5 liters) of mucus every day.

Hair Color: Blonde hair is generally thinner and contains more hair follicles than brown or black hair.

Erections: Men can have erections even while they're in the womb.

Sweat Composition: Sweat itself is odorless; the unpleasant odor comes from bacteria breaking down the sweat on your skin.

Belly Button Lint: The lint that accumulates in your belly button is primarily made up of fibers from your clothing.

Laughing: Laughing increases the production of endorphins, the body's natural painkillers.

Smell Memories: The sense of smell is closely linked to memory and can trigger strong emotional responses.

Tongue Print: Just like fingerprints, every person has a unique tongue print.

Mouth Bacteria: There are more bacteria living in your mouth than there are people on Earth.

Bowel Movements: On average, you'll spend about three years of your life on the toilet.

Finger Length: The length of your fingers is determined by the amount of testosterone you were exposed to in the womb.

Floating Eyeballs: Your eyeballs are buoyant, but they are kept in place by the surrounding muscles and tissue.

Skin Wrinkles: Soaking in water makes your skin wrinkled due to the contraction of blood vessels, not because it absorbs water.

Red Blood Cells: Red blood cells are constantly renewed and have a lifespan of about 120 days.

Belly Button Shape: The shape of your belly button is determined by how your umbilical cord was cut and healed after birth.

Noisy Joints: The cracking sound you hear when you crack your knuckles is caused by the release of gas bubbles in the synovial fluid in your joints.

Fingerprint Evolution: Primates, including humans, developed unique fingerprints to improve grip on wet or slippery surfaces.

Heart Location: The human heart is located in the center of the chest, not on the left side as commonly believed.

Gut Feeling: The gut contains millions of neurons and neurotransmitters, earning it the nickname "the second brain."

Brain Farts: Forgetting what you were going to say is called a "mondegreen."

Sleep Paralysis: During REM sleep, your brain releases chemicals that inhibit muscle movement to prevent you from acting out your dreams. Sleep paralysis occurs when you wake up before these chemicals wear off.

Stomach Acid: Your stomach produces hydrochloric acid, which is strong enough to dissolve a razor blade.

Bone Strength: The bones in your body are stronger than steel in terms of supporting weight, but steel is denser and stronger overall.

Earwax Flavor: Some people can taste the flavor of their earwax.

Nail Growth: Fingernails grow faster than toenails, and nails grow faster on your dominant hand.

Fingerprint Recognition: The ridges on your fingertips help improve grip and make it easier to pick up objects.

Eye Color: The color of your eyes is determined by the amount and type of pigments in your iris.

Lung Size: Your lungs contain about 300 million tiny air sacs called alveoli, with a total surface area equivalent to a tennis court.

Tooth Decay: Tooth enamel is the hardest substance in the human body, but it can still be eroded by acidic foods and drinks.

Kidney Filtration: Your kidneys filter about 200 quarts (190 liters) of blood each day to remove waste and excess water.

Toothprints: Just like fingerprints and tongue prints, dental imprints are unique to each person.

Jaw Strength: The human jaw can exert a force equivalent to 200 pounds of pressure on the molars.

Goatee Growth: Men's facial hair grows faster than any other hair on their bodies.

Belly Button Vortex: The direction in which the hair grows around your belly button forms a vortex pattern unique to each person.

Stomach Size: Your stomach can expand to hold up to 4 liters of food and liquid.

Skin Cells: The surface of your skin is covered in approximately 19 million skin cells.

Swallowing: Swallowing is a complex process that involves about 50 pairs of muscles and takes about 22 seconds from start to finish.

Eyelashes: Eyelashes have an average lifespan of about 150 days.

Hearing Range: The average human can hear sounds in the frequency range of 20 to 20,000 Hertz, but this range diminishes with age.

Gut Microbes: There are trillions of microorganisms living in your gut, collectively known as the gut microbiome.

Teeth Impressions: The alignment and shape of your teeth are as unique as your fingerprints.

Finger Pads: The skin on your fingertips, palms, and soles of your feet has no hair or sweat glands.

Tears Composition: Tears contain three different layers: an outer oily layer, a middle watery layer, and an inner mucous layer.

Voice Changes: Your voice changes throughout the day due to factors like hydration, tiredness, and body temperature.

Breathing Rate: The average person takes about 20,000 breaths in a day.

Facial Muscles: Smiling requires the use of 17 facial muscles, while frowning uses 43.

Nasal Blood Supply: The blood vessels in your nose are capable of expanding and contracting to regulate airflow and temperature.

Nasal Mucus Production: Your nose produces about one quart (approximately one liter) of mucus each day.

Earwax Protection: Earwax, or cerumen, acts as a protective barrier to prevent dust and foreign particles from entering the ear canal.

Temperature Regulation: Your body maintains a core temperature of around 98.6°F (37°C), but this can vary slightly from person to person.

Tooth Sensitivity: The enamel on your teeth is semi-translucent, which is why they can appear slightly yellowish or gray.

Spinal Cord Length: The spinal cord is shorter than the spinal column, so it doesn't extend all the way to the bottom of the spine.

Pain Threshold: The perception of pain varies among individuals, with some people having a higher pain threshold than others.

Muscle Contractions: Muscle contractions can generate more heat than any other bodily function, which can help maintain body temperature.

Hiccup Causes: Hiccups can be triggered by factors like overeating, drinking carbonated beverages, or sudden changes in temperature.

Sweat Gland Density: There are approximately 2-4 million sweat glands on the human body.

Pupil Size: The size of your pupils can change in response to light, emotions, and even attraction.

Nail Growth Rate: Fingernails grow faster than toenails, and the rate of growth can vary depending on factors like age and health.

Temperature Sensitivity: Your skin is sensitive to temperature changes, and it can detect temperature differences as small as 0.036°F (0.02°C).

Heartbeat Sound: The "lub-dub" sound of the heartbeat is created by the closing of heart valves and the rush of blood through the heart's chambers.

Tongue Rolling: The ability to roll your tongue into a tube shape is determined by genetics.

Pregnancy Hormones: During pregnancy, a woman's body produces a hormone called relaxin, which helps relax the uterine muscles but can also affect other joints in the body.

Eyebrow Lifespan: Eyebrows have a lifespan of about four months before they fall out and regrow.

Muscle Tension: The human body has over 600 muscles, and they make up about 40% of a person's total body weight.

Eye Muscles: The muscles that move your eyes are the most active muscles in your body.

Pheromones: Humans release chemical signals called pheromones, which can affect the behavior of others, but their role in human interaction is still debated.

Nail Strength: The hardness of your fingernails is due to the presence of a protein called keratin.

Pheromone Production: Humans produce pheromones not just in sweat but also in their tears and saliva, though their role in human communication is still not fully understood.

Pacemaker Cells: The heart contains special cells called "pacemaker cells" that generate electrical signals to regulate the heartbeat, and they can continue functioning even outside the body.

Fingerprints' Regeneration: If you damage your fingerprints, they will regenerate over time, but they may not return exactly to their original pattern.

Blood Vessels: If you were to line up all the blood vessels in an adult human body, they would stretch for over 60,000 miles (about 97,000 kilometers).

Blinking Lifetime: Over an average lifespan, a person will spend about six months of their life blinking.

Heartbeat Synchronization: When people spend time together, their heartbeats tend to synchronize, even if they are not consciously aware of it.

Hair Count: The average person has about 100,000 to 150,000 hair follicles on their scalp, and the number of hair strands can vary widely among individuals.

HISTORICAL FIGURES

Albert Einstein: Einstein never wore socks, and he often cut the toes off his shoes to let his feet breathe.

Cleopatra: Cleopatra reportedly bathed in milk to maintain her youthful appearance.

Isaac Newton: Newton invented the cat door by cutting two holes in his door so his cats could come and go freely.

Vincent van Gogh: Van Gogh only sold one painting during his lifetime, "The Red Vineyard."

Benjamin Franklin: Franklin was an advocate of "air baths," which involved sitting naked by an open window to improve health.

Genghis Khan: Genghis Khan is believed to have fathered so many children that about 1 in every 200 men alive today is his descendant.

Marie Curie: Curie's notebooks from her pioneering research on radioactivity are still too radioactive to handle safely.

Napoleon Bonaparte: Napoleon was often given a cold bath by his servants because he believed it would invigorate him.

Mark Twain: Twain was born shortly after Halley's Comet appeared in 1835 and predicted he would die when it returned. He died in 1910, the year it reappeared.

Gandhi: Gandhi slept next to young women to test his vow of chastity, believing it would prove his self-control.

Abraham Lincoln: Lincoln was a skilled wrestler, with only one recorded defeat in about 300 matches.

Catherine the Great: Catherine the Great was known for her love of furniture, particularly collecting thousands of chairs.

Charles Darwin: Darwin suffered from chronic health issues and was often seen as a hypochondriac.

Winston Churchill: Churchill had a pet parrot named Charlie, who often mimicked his voice and squawked obscenities.

Mozart: Mozart had an unusual sense of humor and wrote a piece called "Lick My Ass" as a child.

Queen Victoria: Queen Victoria proposed to her future husband, Prince Albert, rather than the other way around.

Pablo Picasso: Picasso's full name was Pablo Diego José Francisco de Paula Juan Nepomuceno María de los Remedios Cipriano de la Santísima Trinidad Ruiz y Picasso.

George Washington: Washington's false teeth were not made of wood but were crafted from a combination of materials, including human teeth, animal teeth, and ivory.

Julius Caesar: Caesar was kidnapped by pirates as a young man. He reportedly joked with them that he would come back and crucify them, which he later did after being freed.

Beethoven: Beethoven was known to count coffee beans for his daily brew: 60 beans per cup.

Amelia Earhart: Earhart used to sleep in her pilot's jacket to get accustomed to the smell of aviation fuel.

Sigmund Freud: Freud had an intense fear of ferns, known as "pteridophobia."

Rasputin: Rasputin survived multiple assassination attempts, including poisoning, shooting, and drowning.

Casanova: Giacomo Casanova, the famous lover, was also a prolific writer and wrote a 12-volume autobiography.

Mata Hari: Mata Hari, the exotic dancer and spy, was executed by firing squad during World War I.

Queen Elizabeth I: Queen Elizabeth I had a pet sugar glider, a small marsupial from Australia.

Sir Isaac Newton: Newton invented the cat door to let his cat, Spithead, in and out of his study while he worked.

Eleanor Roosevelt: Roosevelt kept a pet snake named Emily Spinach in the White House.

Pope Gregory IX: In the 13th century, Pope Gregory IX declared war on cats, believing they were associated with witchcraft.

Franklin Pierce: The 14th U.S. President, Franklin Pierce, accidentally ran over and killed a woman with his horse during his presidency.

Rasputin: Rasputin, the Russian mystic, is rumored to have survived poisoning, drowning, and being shot multiple times before his eventual murder.

Benjamin Franklin: Franklin wrote an essay titled "Fart Proudly" in which he argued for the health benefits of passing gas.

Leonardo da Vinci: Da Vinci was known for writing his notes backward, a technique called "mirror writing," to protect his ideas from theft.

Marie Antoinette: Marie Antoinette's extravagant spending on fashion and parties contributed to the financial crisis in France.

Nero: Roman Emperor Nero was said to have played the fiddle while Rome burned, though this account is disputed by historians.

Caligula: Caligula, another Roman Emperor, is known for his bizarre and often cruel behavior, including making his horse a senator.

Marie Curie: Curie carried test tubes of radioactive isotopes in her pocket and stored them in her desk, leading to radiation exposure.

Thomas Edison: Edison was afraid of the dark and often slept with the lights on.

Fidel Castro: Castro survived over 600 assassination attempts during his time as Cuba's leader.

Charles Dickens: Dickens had an obsession with arranging objects in his home in precise geometric patterns.

Alexander the Great: Alexander the Great was tutored by Aristotle and carried the philosopher's works with him during his military campaigns.

Coco Chanel: Chanel was superstitious and believed that the number 5 was lucky, leading to the creation of Chanel No. 5 perfume.

Pope John XII: John XII, a pope in the 10th century, was so corrupt that he was accused of turning the Vatican into a brothel.

King Tutankhamun: King Tut's tomb contained a dagger made from meteorite iron, a rare and precious material at the time.

Joan of Arc: Joan of Arc claimed to have heard the voices of saints, which inspired her to lead the French army during the Hundred Years' War.

Alexander Graham Bell: Bell's mother and wife were both deaf, which influenced his work on the telephone.

Hans Christian Andersen: Andersen was known to be socially awkward and once attended a party at Charles Dickens' house, where he overstayed his welcome for five weeks.

Harriet Tubman: Tubman, a former slave and abolitionist, was also a spy for the Union Army during the Civil War.

Nellie Bly: Journalist Nellie Bly traveled around the world in 72 days, inspired by Jules Verne's novel "Around the World in Eighty Days."

William Shakespeare: Shakespeare's cause of death remains a mystery, and there are many theories, including one that suggests he died from a drinking binge with fellow playwrights.

Napoleon Bonaparte: Napoleon was known for his fondness for short leaders and once had a personal guard composed of very tall soldiers, known as the "Long Guard."

Pocahontas: Pocahontas, the Native American woman who famously interacted with English colonists, was eventually taken to England, where she was presented as a curiosity at various events.

George Washington: Washington had a lifelong fear of being buried alive, so he requested that his body be left untouched for three days after his death.

Cleopatra: Cleopatra spoke several languages fluently, including Greek, Egyptian, and Latin.

Andy Warhol: Warhol often used cats as subjects in his artwork, including his famous painting of "25 Cats Named Sam and One Blue Pussy."

Frida Kahlo: Kahlo had a menagerie of pets, including monkeys, parrots, and a deer, which often appeared in her self-portraits.

Wolfgang Amadeus Mozart: Mozart had an unusual sense of humor and wrote a series of humorous compositions, including a piece called "A Musical Joke."

Helen Keller: Keller was not only a remarkable advocate for the deaf and blind but also a suffragette and author. She was the first deaf and blind person to earn a bachelor's degree.

Genghis Khan: Genghis Khan's real name was Temüjin, and he earned the title "Genghis Khan," meaning "universal ruler," after uniting the Mongol tribes.

Galileo Galilei: Galileo once conducted an experiment by dropping objects of different weights from the Leaning Tower of Pisa to demonstrate that they would fall at the same rate.

Catherine de' Medici: Catherine de' Medici, a queen of France, was known for her love of perfumes and is credited with popularizing the use of perfume in Europe.

Florence Nightingale: Nightingale was not just a nurse but also a prolific writer and statistician, and she invented a kind of pie chart called the "rose diagram."

George Orwell: Orwell, the author of "1984" and "Animal Farm," was known for his love of gardening and kept a diary about his experiences.

Grace Hopper: Hopper, a computer scientist, coined the term "debugging" when she removed a moth from a computer relay.

Marilyn Monroe: Monroe had an IQ of 168 and was a voracious reader, despite her "dumb blonde" persona.

Marquis de Sade: The term "sadism" is derived from the Marquis de

Sade's name due to his infamous writings on sexual cruelty.

Ernest Hemingway: Hemingway survived multiple plane crashes in his lifetime and once survived a brush with death in a car accident involving a bazooka.

Jane Austen: Austen initially wrote her novels anonymously and was known as "A Lady" on the title pages.

Alexander the Great: Alexander once solved a dispute between two men over a dog by offering to buy the dog and give it to the first man, while the second man received a sum of money equal to the dog's value.

Queen Victoria: Queen Victoria had a pet African Grey parrot named Coco that could mimic her husband Prince Albert's voice and swear in several languages.

Mao Zedong: Mao Zedong was known for his love of swimming in the Yangtze River and used to lead group swims with his political allies.

Thomas Jefferson: Jefferson designed his own tombstone and requested that it list his accomplishments as an author of the Declaration of Independence and the Virginia Statute for Religious Freedom, but omitted his presidency.

Christopher Columbus: Columbus believed he had reached Asia when he arrived in the Americas, and he died still believing he had discovered a western route to Asia.

Rosa Parks: Before her famous act of civil disobedience, Rosa Parks worked as a seamstress and a cook, and she was also a member of the NAACP.

Vlad the Impaler: The real-life inspiration for Dracula, Vlad the Impaler, was notorious for his cruel methods of torture and execution, which often involved impaling his victims on wooden stakes.

Catherine the Great: Catherine the Great of Russia had a voracious appetite for reading and amassed one of the largest private libraries in the world.

Emily Dickinson: The famous poet Emily Dickinson rarely left her home and was known for her reclusive lifestyle.

Joan of Arc: Joan of Arc claimed to hear voices of saints from a young age, which she believed were guiding her.

Walt Disney: Walt Disney was afraid of mice, which is ironic given that one of his most iconic characters is Mickey Mouse.

William the Conqueror: William the Conqueror, who famously led the Norman Conquest of England, was so overweight that his body burst when it was placed in a stone sarcophagus during his funeral.

Benjamin Disraeli: Disraeli, a British Prime Minister, is the only British Prime Minister to have been of Jewish descent.

Margaret Thatcher: Margaret Thatcher, the "Iron Lady" of British politics, had a degree in chemistry.

Rosa Parks: Rosa Parks' refusal to give up her bus seat to a white person sparked the Montgomery Bus Boycott, a key event in the

American Civil Rights Movement.

Henry VIII: King Henry VIII of England had six wives and is known for his role in the English Reformation.

Vincent van Gogh: Van Gogh famously cut off his own ear during a bout of mental illness.

Emily Brontë: Emily Brontë, author of "Wuthering Heights," used the pen name "Ellis Bell" when publishing her works.

Benjamin Franklin: Franklin had a deep love for air baths and believed that spending time nude and ventilated could improve one's health.

Eleanor Roosevelt: Eleanor Roosevelt was the first First Lady to hold press conferences and write a daily newspaper column.

Socrates: Socrates was a philosopher known for his method of questioning, the Socratic method, which is still used in education today.

Hedy Lamarr: The actress Hedy Lamarr co-invented an early version of frequency hopping technology, which contributed to the development of modern wireless communication.

John F. Kennedy: President Kennedy was an avid speed reader and could reportedly read about 1,200 words per minute.

Salvador Dalí: Dalí often used ants as a symbol in his artwork, fascinated by their segmented bodies and the idea of decay.

Leonardo da Vinci: Leonardo da Vinci was a vegetarian and

advocated for the ethical treatment of animals.

Marie Antoinette: Marie Antoinette's lavish spending on fashion and jewelry earned her the nickname "Madame Deficit."

Sylvia Plath: Sylvia Plath, the poet and novelist, was also an accomplished artist and illustrator.

Ernest Hemingway: Hemingway wrote standing up because he believed it improved his writing.

Agatha Christie: Agatha Christie, the famous mystery author, once mysteriously disappeared for 11 days, leading to speculation about her whereabouts.

Hannibal Barca: The Carthaginian general Hannibal Barca famously crossed the Alps with his army, including war elephants, to attack Rome.

Pierre Curie: Pierre Curie, the husband of Marie Curie, died in a street accident when he slipped and fell, leading to a carriage running over his head.

Helen Keller: Helen Keller was the first deafblind person to earn a Bachelor of Arts degree.

Gustav Eiffel: Gustav Eiffel, the engineer behind the Eiffel Tower, designed a moveable observatory that was used to study the solar eclipse in 1889.

Charlie Chaplin: Charlie Chaplin once entered a Charlie Chaplin look-alike contest and came in third place.

Hedy Lamarr: In addition to her contributions to wireless technology, Hedy Lamarr was also an inventor of a tablet that would dissolve in water to create a carbonated drink.

Gustave Eiffel: Gustave Eiffel also designed the internal structure of the Statue of Liberty in New York City.

BOOKS

The Library of Congress in the United States is the largest library in the world, with over 170 million items in its collection.

"The Guinness Book of World Records" holds the record for being the most stolen book from public libraries.

One of the earliest pop-up books, "The Movables," was created in 1843 by Lothar Meggendorfer and featured intricate paper engineering.

The Barnes & Noble bookstore in New York City's Union Square is considered the world's largest bookstore, spanning over 154,250 square feet.

The Japanese have a word for the act of acquiring books and letting them pile up, unread. It's called "tsundoku."

A British author legally changed his name to "Captain Fantastic Faster Than Superman Spiderman Batman Wolverine Hulk And The Flash Combined" to fit it on his book covers.

The World Book Throwing Championships is a real event where participants throw books as far as they can. It takes place in a small Welsh town.

Johannes Gutenberg's Bible, printed in the 15th century, is considered the first major book printed with movable type.

"Remembrance of Things Past" by Marcel Proust is one of the longest novels ever written, with over 1.5 million words.

Some bookstores and libraries offer wristbands that allow you to scan books' barcodes, so you can remember titles you want to read later.

The term "blurb" was coined by author Gelett Burgess in 1907 when he wrote a positive review for his own book and featured it on the back cover.

The Livraria Lello in Porto, Portugal, is a bookstore famous for its stunning architecture and was said to have inspired J.K. Rowling while writing the Harry Potter series.

"Bibliosmia" is the word for the scent of a good book, and it's a term many book lovers can relate to.

Some used books contain interesting annotations or marginalia made by previous readers, creating a unique historical record.

The "Diamond Sutra," a Buddhist text printed in China in 868 AD, is considered the oldest surviving printed book.

A practice known as anthropodermic bibliopegy involved binding books with human skin. Some examples exist in rare book collections.

The longest sentence in literature is in the book "The Rotters' Club" by Jonathan Coe, with a sentence that spans 13,955 words.

There's a book titled "The Great Emu War" that documents the strange historical event when the Australian military faced off against emus.

NASA left a book on the moon during the Apollo 15 mission. It's called the "Fallen Astronaut" and contains the names of 14 astronauts who had died at the time.

The most expensive book ever sold at auction is Leonardo da Vinci's notebook, known as the "Codex Leicester," which sold for over $30 million.

NAMES

The longest personal name ever recorded belonged to a man named Hubert Wolfeschlegelsteinhausenbergerdorff. His full name had 988 letters.

Some countries, like Sweden, have strict naming laws that prohibit names that might cause offense or be considered inappropriate.

New Zealand has banned names like "Lucifer," "Mafia No Fear," "4Real," and "V8" because they don't comply with naming regulations.

The fear of long words is called "hippopotomonstrosesquipedaliophobia," which is ironic given its long name.

Some names, like "Hannah" and "Anna," are palindromic, meaning they read the same forwards and backwards.

Some celebrities, like Madonna and Cher, are so iconic that they're known by a single name.

In some countries, people take surnames based on their occupation. For example, "Smith" was often used for blacksmiths.

Surnames were first introduced in England during the Middle Ages to help identify individuals with similar first names.

In 1993, the musician Prince changed his name to an unpronounceable symbol, leading to him being referred to as "The Artist Formerly Known as Prince."

The letter "J" is one of the newest additions to the English alphabet, appearing around the 16th century.

Many authors use pseudonyms or pen names, such as George Orwell (real name Eric Blair) and Mark Twain (real name Samuel Clemens).

The first person to join Facebook after Mark Zuckerberg was Arie Hasit, a Facebook intern.

The name "Google" was a misspelling of "googol," which is a mathematical term representing the number 1 followed by 100 zeros.

Some names are tongue twisters, like "She sells seashells by the seashore," which is inspired by the real-life Mary Anning.

Some people change their names in the belief that it will bring them better luck or fortune.

The name "Alice" is often used in literature, appearing as the main character in Lewis Carroll's "Alice's Adventures in Wonderland" and in "Alice Through the Looking-Glass."

Celebrities are known for giving their children unique names, like "North West" (Kim Kardashian and Kanye West's daughter) and

"Apple" (Gwyneth Paltrow and Chris Martin's daughter).

The most common first name in the world is "Muhammad," followed by variations like "Mohammed" and "Mohammad."

Filmmakers sometimes use fake names in scripts to prevent leaks and spoilers, leading to rumors and speculation among fans.

"John Smith" is often used as a generic name in English-speaking countries due to its commonality.

Similar to "Jane Doe," "John Doe" is a placeholder name for an unidentified or generic male in legal contexts.

Some parents name their children after celebrities, leading to trends in baby names. For example, the name "Beyoncé" saw a spike in popularity after the singer's rise to fame.

"Li" is the most common surname in the world, primarily due to its prevalence in China.

In some families, names are passed down through generations, leading to multiple individuals with the same name, often distinguished by Roman numerals (e.g., John Smith III).

Some names can be challenging to pronounce correctly, leading to humorous mispronunciations and nicknames.

Different cultures have unique naming customs and traditions, such as the use of patronymic or matronymic names.

"Anonymous" is a common name used online when people want to remain unidentified or pseudonymous.

Many entertainers adopt stage names for various reasons, such as creating a distinct persona or for privacy. For example, "Lady Gaga" is a stage name for Stefani Joanne Angelina Germanotta.

"Mary" is one of the most popular names in history, and variations like "Maria" are common in many cultures.

Some nicknames have interesting origins. For example, "Dick" is a nickname for "Richard," and "Peggy" comes from "Margaret."

The popularity of the "Harry Potter" series led to a surge in the name "Harry" for newborns.

The study of names, their origins, and meanings is called "onomastics."

Royal families often have strict naming traditions, with names passed down through generations. For example, multiple British monarchs have been named "George."

Some people are named after brands or products, like a Swedish couple who named their child "Ikea" after the furniture store.

Some parents name their children after places they have fond memories of or places they find significant.

Names go in and out of fashion, with some names experiencing revivals after decades of obscurity.

Some names, like "Taylor" or "Jordan," are considered unisex and can be given to people of any gender.

"Qwerty" is the name of the standard keyboard layout, and some parents have chosen it as a unique name for their children.

After the character "Seven of Nine" in the TV series "Star Trek: Voyager," some parents have given their children the name "Seven."

MUSIC

In the 1930s, scientists attempted to turn beans into a musical instrument by embedding them with small radio transmitters. It was an early attempt at creating edible music.

The longest continuous concert lasted 240 hours and was performed by various artists in Canada in 2009.

The heaviest naturally occurring element on Earth, uranium, has a chemical symbol of "U," which some have humorously referred to as the most "metal" symbol on the periodic table.

The largest orchestra ever assembled had 7,548 participants and was achieved in Mumbai, India, in 2019.

In 2015, astronaut Chris Hadfield recorded an album aboard the International Space Station, making it the first album partially recorded in space.

Beethoven was known to count out exactly 60 coffee beans for his morning coffee, believing it would provide him with the perfect cup.

For years, "Happy Birthday to You" was under copyright protection, making it technically illegal to sing it in public without permission. The copyright was eventually invalidated.

The tritone, an interval of three whole tones, was once referred to as the "Devil's Interval" in medieval music due to its dissonant sound.

A metal band in Australia named itself "The Great Emu War Casualties" in homage to the bizarre historical event when the Australian military fought against emus.

The cover of the Beatles' "Sgt. Pepper's Lonely Hearts Club Band" album features the image of Aleister Crowley, a controversial occultist and magician, among other historical figures.

The "brown note" is a fictional sound frequency that supposedly causes people to lose control of their bowels. It's a popular urban legend.

The secret behind the extraordinary sound of Stradivarius violins, made by Antonio Stradivari in the 17th and 18th centuries, remains a subject of debate and fascination among musicians and scientists.

Studies have shown that the type of music played while drinking wine can influence how the wine tastes.

Contrary to the children's rhyme, beans are not inherently musical, but they can cause gas in some individuals.

There's a city ordinance in Santa Clara, California, that makes it illegal to whistle for a lost canary before 7 AM.

Wolfgang Amadeus Mozart composed a piece of music called "Leck mich im Arsch," which translates to "Lick Me in the Arse." It's a humorous canon.

Queen's "Bohemian Rhapsody" was the first music video ever made and is considered one of the greatest rock songs of all time.

The phrase "playing the world's smallest violin" is used humorously to mock someone complaining about minor issues.

The B-52s' song "Rock Lobster" was responsible for the discovery of a new species of lobster, which was named "Kiwa puravida."

In 1951, the first computer-generated music was produced by a computer called the CSIRAC in Australia.

In the 1960s, the Beach Boys' Brian Wilson hired a musician named Carol Kaye to play bass guitar on many of the band's recordings. However, she was never credited, leading to her being referred to as the "Phantom Bass Player."

The internet phenomenon known as "Rickrolling" involves tricking someone into clicking a hyperlink that leads to the music video for Rick Astley's "Never Gonna Give You Up."

A company in Japan developed a tiny karaoke machine that is the size of a matchbox.

Musicians created a piece called the "Most Unwanted Song" based on a survey of people's musical dislikes. It includes bagpipes, children singing about holidays, and a tuba.

A Canadian dentist purchased John Lennon's tooth at an auction for over $31,000 in 2011.

The theremin is one of the world's earliest electronic instruments and is played without physical contact. It's known for its eerie, otherworldly sound.

The opening chord of the Beatles' song "A Hard Day's Night" has been the subject of much debate and analysis among musicians.

The record for the most concerts performed in 24 hours by a single artist is held by Hunter Hayes, who performed ten concerts in 24 hours in 2014.

The world's largest drum kit featured over 1,000 individual drums and cymbals and was played by 813 drummers simultaneously in India.

The comedy group "The Lonely Island" is known for creating viral music videos, including "I'm On A Boat" and "Dick in a Box."

The famous "Jaws" theme song, composed by John Williams, is often used to create tension and humor in various media.

The kazoo, a simple musical instrument, has occasionally been used in classical compositions.

"The Chicken Dance" is a popular novelty song that's often played at weddings and other celebrations. It's also known as the "Birdie Song."

Some musicians have incorporated recordings of whale songs into their compositions, creating a unique blend of natural and musical sounds.

The "William Tell Overture" is frequently used in humorous and action-packed scenes in movies and television shows.

A singing Tesla coil is a musical instrument that produces music by modulating the sparks of electrical discharges from the coil.

Some fictional bands from movies and TV shows, like "Spinal Tap" and "The Monkees," have gained popularity in the real world.

The theremin's eerie sound is often used in science fiction movie soundtracks to create an otherworldly atmosphere.

Gilbert and Sullivan's comic operas, like "The Pirates of Penzance" and "The Mikado," are known for their humor and witty lyrics.

David DiDonato holds the record for the longest guitar solo, lasting 24 hours, 18 minutes, and 15 seconds.

The novelty Christmas song "Grandma Got Run Over by a Reindeer" was written by a husband-and-wife duo, Randy and Elmo Shropshire, as a joke.

Some toothbrushes are designed to play music for two minutes, the recommended time for brushing teeth.

The humorous song "Chicken Attack" by Schmoyoho gained popularity on the internet and features a catchy chorus about chickens attacking.

"It's the End of the World as We Know It (And I Feel Fine)" by R.E.M. is known for its rapid-fire lyrics and has been used in many movies and TV shows.

Whistling is used as a musical element in some songs, such as "Young Folks" by Peter Bjorn and John.

The Kazoo Symphony Orchestra is a real orchestra that uses kazoos as their primary instruments to play classical and popular music.

Many popular songs are built on just three chords, making them relatively easy to play on various instruments.

There's a humorous reference in music to the "Lost Chord," which is a mythical, perfect musical chord that has been sought after by composers for centuries.

In 2013, 7,224 people in China set a world record for the largest musical ensemble, playing traditional Chinese instruments.

NASA has recorded and released the sounds of space, including the eerie sounds of Saturn's rings and the "sounds" of distant galaxies.

In 1968, a piano was dropped from a helicopter 80 feet in the air as an artistic experiment, resulting in a cacophonous crash.

The distinctive whistling theme from many Spaghetti Western films has become iconic in its own right.

The Rubber Chicken Orchestra: Some musicians and comedians use rubber chickens as musical instruments, playing them by squeezing and bending them to create sounds.

Mozart composed a humorous canon titled "Leck mich im Arsch," which translates to "Lick Me in the Arse."

"Yakety Sax," also known as the "Benny Hill Theme," is often used in comedic videos to accompany humorous chase scenes.

In Lancaster, California, there's a road with grooves that play the William Tell Overture when cars drive over them at the correct speed.

NASA's Mars rover Curiosity played the song "Happy Birthday" to itself on its first anniversary of landing on Mars.

The Music of Whales: The songs of humpback whales have been studied and even incorporated into new age music.

MOVIES

A stock sound effect known as the "Wilhelm Scream" has been used in over 400 films, including "Star Wars" and "Indiana Jones."

"Fresh Guacamole" is a stop-motion animated film that's just over a minute long. It was nominated for an Academy Award.

Fans spotted Starbucks coffee cups mistakenly left in a scene of "Game of Thrones," leading to jokes and memes.

The famous "Here's Johnny!" scene in "The Shining" took 127 takes, a record in filmmaking.

The White House is often destroyed in disaster movies. It's been blown up, invaded, and even destroyed by aliens in various films.

The film "The Room," often considered one of the worst movies ever made, has gained a cult following with midnight screenings and fan participation.

In the film "127 Hours," James Franco's character cuts off his arm. A prosthetic arm and camera tricks were used to create the gruesome effect.

The "Sharknado" film series features tornadoes filled with sharks and has become known for its over-the-top absurdity.

The concept of movie trailers originated when a New York-based theater owner played a short film advertising his upcoming movie, "The Great Train Robbery," in 1909.

The film "The Adventures of Priscilla, Queen of the Desert" holds the record for the most costume changes in a single film, with 50 costume changes.

In "Groundhog Day," Bill Murray's character took 101 takes to get the word "What?" just right.

The 1964 Chevrolet Chevelle Malibu used in "Pulp Fiction" was stolen during the film's production and was missing for nearly two decades.

"The Artist," a modern silent film, won the Academy Award for Best Picture in 2012, the first silent film to do so since the original Oscars in 1929.

The Philadelphia Museum of Art's steps are known as the "Rocky Steps" because of the iconic scene in "Rocky" where Sylvester Stallone runs up them.

The T. rex roar in "Jurassic Park" was created by combining the sounds of a baby elephant, a tiger, and an alligator.

The Pizza Planet delivery truck from "Toy Story" makes appearances in nearly every Pixar film, becoming an Easter egg for fans.

In "Home Alone," the paint cans used as weapons by Macaulay Culkin were actually filled with pillows to avoid injuring the actors.

The sound in the film "Inception" is inspired by the slowed-down, distorted version of Edith Piaf's song "Non, Je Ne Regrette Rien."

The film "Meet Joe Black" holds the record for the most on-screen deaths, with 58 deaths depicted in a single movie.

The famous parade scene in "Ferris Bueller's Day Off" was not originally planned but was added after a real parade took place during filming.

The original Godzilla suit in the 1954 film was so heavy and hot that the actor inside it passed out from heat exhaustion during takes.

The famous bean-eating scene in "Blazing Saddles" featured the actors consuming real beans, which led to unexpected consequences on set.

In "The Wizard of Oz," the horse that changes color in the Emerald City was covered in Jell-O crystals to achieve the effect.

In "Terminator 2: Judgment Day," Arnold Schwarzenegger's stunt double looks so much like him that even Schwarzenegger's own mother couldn't tell them apart in a photo.

The sounds of the Velociraptors in "Jurassic Park" were created by blending the cries of tortoises mating and the sounds of a walrus.

The scene in "The Dark Knight" where Heath Ledger's Joker claps in jail was unscripted. Ledger's applause was genuine and added to the film.

In "Star Wars: Episode IV - A New Hope," a stormtrooper famously hits his head on a door frame. The mistake was left in the film.

Actor Harrison Ford has a fear of snakes, yet he had to film many scenes with them in "Raiders of the Lost Ark."

Jack Nicholson's character in "The Shining" types "All work and no play makes Jack a dull boy" repeatedly. The pages seen in the movie were all individually typed by Kubrick's secretary.

In "E.T. the Extra-Terrestrial," there's a scene where E.T. sees a child dressed as Yoda from "Star Wars" and says, "Home." This suggests a connection between the two film universes.

The "Death's-head Hawkmoth" featured in "The Silence of the Lambs" is not native to the United States and had to be imported for the film.

The giant Stay Puft Marshmallow Man in "Ghostbusters" was originally supposed to be a giant devil but was changed to be less frightening.

In "Jaws," the scene where Roy Scheider examines a shark's head was actually filmed with a real, dead shark.

The river in the chocolate room of Willy Wonka's factory in "Charlie and the Chocolate Factory" was made of 15,000 gallons of actual chocolate.

The famous "bullet time" effect in "The Matrix" was created by using multiple still cameras, not high-speed filming.

The contents of the briefcase in "Pulp Fiction" are never revealed, leading to endless fan theories about what's inside.

Mike Myers originally recorded all of Shrek's lines in a Canadian accent but later re-recorded them in a Scottish accent after finding it funnier.

The original concept for the time machine in "Back to the Future" was a refrigerator, but it was changed to the iconic DeLorean car.

The green falling code in "The Matrix" is a combination of Japanese sushi recipes and symbols from the Bible.

To create E.T.'s voice, sound designer Ben Burtt recorded the sounds of raccoons, sea otters, and other animals.

During the filming of "The Lord of the Rings" trilogy, several actors sustained injuries. Viggo Mortensen broke two toes kicking a helmet, and Orlando Bloom broke a rib falling off a horse.

The creators of the animated TV series "The Real Ghostbusters" had to add "Real" to the title because of a lawsuit from the creators of the original "Ghostbusters" film.

The trolley scene in "Harry Potter and the Sorcerer's Stone," where the trolley is pushed through the wall at Platform 9¾, was achieved by having crew members physically push the trolley through a wall.

Tom Hardy's portrayal of Bane in "The Dark Knight Rises" was originally criticized for being difficult to understand. As a result, the audio had to be reworked in post-production to make Bane's voice clearer.

Stanley Kubrick originally filmed a massive pie fight scene for "Dr. Strangelove," but it was cut from the final film.

The actors in "The Blair Witch Project" were not credited with their real names in order to maintain the illusion that the film was a real documentary.

The famous airport scene in "Casablanca" was filmed entirely on a soundstage with a small model airplane and midgets as extras to create the illusion of a crowded airport.

In "Grease," John Travolta was 24 years old when he played a high school student, while Olivia Newton-John was 29.

During the filming of "The Exorcist," a fire destroyed the set, and the actress who played Regan's mother, Ellen Burstyn, suffered a permanent back injury when a stunt went wrong.

The famous line "Mrs. Robinson, you're trying to seduce me, aren't you?" in "The Graduate" was ad-libbed by Dustin Hoffman.

"Clerks," directed by Kevin Smith, was shot in the actual convenience store where Smith worked, using the store's stock of snacks and beverages.

Arnold Schwarzenegger's thick Austrian accent led to some humorous mispronunciations. In "The Terminator," he originally pronounced "I'll be back" as "I'll be bahk."

The famous line "I am your father" in "The Empire Strikes Back" was kept a secret from the cast and crew until the day of filming to preserve the surprise.

During the filming of "Predator," there was a bodybuilding competition between Arnold Schwarzenegger, Carl Weathers, and other cast members.

Harrison Ford has a fear of snakes, yet he had to film scenes with them in "Raiders of the Lost Ark." A glass plane separated him from the snakes.

The iconic "Bohemian Rhapsody" scene in "Wayne's World" was almost cut from the film, but it became one of the most memorable moments.

Steve McQueen's famous motorcycle jump in "The Great Escape" was performed by his stunt double, Bud Ekins.

The famous opening crawl in "Star Wars" was created using practical effects. The text was written on a large piece of black paper and filmed using a camera on a track.

To achieve the famous shot of Scarlett O'Hara in her green dress in "Gone with the Wind," the actress wore a special undergarment called a "restraint."

In "Home Alone," the paint can on a string swung at actor Daniel Stern's face. To make it safe, the first swing was stopped just short of hitting him, and the impact was achieved on the second take.

CARTOONS

The animated series "Rocko's Modern Life" often included hidden messages and adult humor that only became apparent to viewers as they got older.

"The Simpsons" is known for predicting various real-world events, including the discovery of the Higgs boson particle and the outcome of Super Bowl games.

The Teenage Mutant Ninja Turtles were initially created as a parody comic of dark and gritty superhero comics of the 1980s.

In the early episodes of "The Flintstones," the characters were seen smoking. These scenes were later edited out due to concerns about smoking's impact on children.

The iconic theme music for "The Pink Panther" was composed by Henry Mancini and is instantly recognizable worldwide.

The character of Bugs Bunny got his name from the catchphrase "What's up, doc?" and was originally called "Bugs' Bunny" as a nod to the animator Ben "Bugs" Hardaway.

The character Shaggy from "Scooby-Doo" was inspired by the character Maynard G. Krebs from the 1950s TV show "The Many Loves of Dobie Gillis."

"South Park" episodes are famously produced in just six days, allowing the show to comment on current events with remarkable speed.

The animated series "The Fairly OddParents" spawned several live-action television movies featuring real actors alongside the animated characters.

Bart Simpson's endorsement of Butterfinger candy bars in the 1990s led to the famous catchphrase, "Nobody better lay a finger on my Butterfinger!"

"Beavis and Butt-Head" faced controversy and criticism for allegedly inspiring destructive behavior among viewers.

Scrooge McDuck, the wealthy character from "DuckTales," is known for his vast wealth. According to Forbes, he would be one of the richest fictional characters if he were real.

The name "Pikachu" is a combination of two Japanese onomatopoeic words: "pika," which represents the sound of electricity, and "chu," which mimics the sound of a mouse's squeak.

"Adventure Time" is filled with hidden references to pop culture, philosophy, and even real-world historical events.

In every episode of "Bob's Burgers," there's a unique "Burger of the Day" listed on the chalkboard outside the restaurant, often with punny and humorous names.

"Gravity Falls" creator Alex Hirsch included various cryptograms and ciphers throughout the show for fans to decode.

"Avatar: The Last Airbender" draws inspiration from Eastern philosophies, martial arts, and mythology, adding depth to its storytelling.

"My Little Pony: Friendship Is Magic" gained an unexpected adult following, often referred to as "Bronies" (bro + ponies).

The fictional city of Townsville in "The Powerpuff Girls" is named after creator Craig McCracken's hometown of Townsville, North Carolina.

"Tom and Jerry" is known for its lack of spoken dialogue, relying on physical comedy and music for storytelling.

Hanna-Barbera licensed Flintstones-themed vitamins, which became one of the most popular children's vitamin brands in the United States.

The location of Springfield in "The Simpsons" has remained deliberately ambiguous throughout the series, leading to various fan theories about its real-world counterpart.

"The Jetsons" featured many futuristic inventions that later became reality, such as video calling, flat-screen TVs, and robot vacuums.

The show's creators, Bryan Konietzko and Michael Dante DiMartino, created a complete alphabet for the "Avatar" universe called "Glossary of Terms."

In real life, Chemical X is a brand name for a line of cleaning products, which is quite different from the mysterious substance that created the Powerpuff Girls.

Velma, the bespectacled member of the Scooby gang, has been known to lose her glasses. This often leads to the famous line, "My glasses! I can't see without my glasses!"

"Futurama" created an entirely new alien language, called "Alienese," which can be deciphered by viewers to reveal hidden jokes and messages.

In the early seasons of "Rugrats," the parents' faces were rarely shown in full. This added an element of mystery to the show.

A "lost" episode of "Dexter's Laboratory" titled "Rude Removal" was created but never aired on television due to its explicit content.

"The Simpsons" holds the record as the longest-running American sitcom, with over 30 seasons and still going strong.

The creator of "Bob's Burgers," Loren Bouchard, developed actual burger recipes for each "Burger of the Day" featured in the show.

The episode titled "The Tower" from "Adventure Time" was temporarily banned in several countries due to its darker themes.

The "My Little Pony" fandom produced an enormous amount of fan-made content, including music, art, and even conventions.

"South Park" episodes are known for their quick turnaround. An episode can be written, animated, and aired in less than a week.

The show's reference to McDonald's Szechuan dipping sauce caused a real-world demand for it, resulting in McDonald's briefly bringing it back.

"Teen Titans Go!" often pokes fun at its own continuity issues, with characters commenting on the show's episodic and nonsensical nature.

The fictional band "Love Händel" from "Phineas and Ferb" performed live at Comic-Con, complete with an album release.

"The Ren & Stimpy Show" often featured dark and risqué humor, pushing the boundaries of what was acceptable for children's animation.

The secret formula for the Krabby Patty has never been revealed, adding to the show's ongoing mystery.

The classic "Tom and Jerry" series won seven Academy Awards for Best Animated Short Subject.

Scrooge McDuck's Number One Dime, the first coin he ever earned, is a central element of his character's backstory in "DuckTales."

The Jetsons' dog, Astro, was named after the futuristic Jet Propulsion Laboratory (JPL) that was active during the show's creation.

"My Little Pony: Friendship Is Magic" featured celebrity voice cameos, including John de Lancie as Discord and "Weird Al" Yankovic as Cheese Sandwich.

The show "Futurama" featured mathematical theorems and equations created by the show's writing team, many of which are legitimate mathematical concepts.

"Rick and Morty" often includes hidden messages and references to future episodes, leading fans to speculate about the show's intricate continuity.

Over the years, "Scooby-Doo" has featured guest appearances by real-life celebrities, including Don Knotts, Dick Van Dyke, and even Batman and Robin.

"Gravity Falls" is known for its cryptic codes hidden in the episodes, some of which required fans to work together to decipher.

The world of "Avatar: The Last Airbender" draws inspiration from various Asian cultures, including Chinese martial arts, Tibetan Buddhism, and Inuit traditions.

The opening credits of "Bob's Burgers" feature a rotating series of punny storefronts next to the restaurant.

The original "Teenage Mutant Ninja Turtles" comics were much darker and grittier than the animated series, featuring more intense violence and mature themes.

"The Fairly OddParents" aired a special episode titled "Fairly OddBaby," which was watched by over 8 million viewers when it premiered.

After being canceled, "Family Guy" was brought back due to strong DVD sales and high ratings in syndication.

The Powerpuff Girls' distinctive outfits and color schemes have inspired fashion collections and designer clothing lines.

"Rugrats" received a spin-off series titled "All Grown Up!" that followed the characters as teenagers.

"SpongeBob SquarePants: The Broadway Musical" received multiple Tony Award nominations and featured original songs by various artists.

The creators of "Tom and Jerry," William Hanna and Joseph Barbera, drew inspiration from silent film comedians like Charlie Chaplin and Buster Keaton.

Many real bands and musicians have appeared on "The Simpsons," including The Beatles, Aerosmith, and Green Day.

"South Park" has tackled controversial subjects and current events, often sparking discussions and even influencing political debates.

CARS

The first speeding ticket was issued in 1902 when a car was caught going 45 mph in a 15 mph zone.

The world's shortest street is only 6 feet long and is called "Elgin Street" in Scotland. It's too short for cars to drive on.

In South Africa, there's a car guarding profession where people watch over parked cars in exchange for tips.

The average car has over 30,000 parts.

The world's slowest car, the Peel P50, has a top speed of 28 mph.

The record for the most people crammed into a Smart car is 19.

The "new car smell" is composed of over 50 volatile organic compounds.

The first recorded car accident occurred in 1891, and it involved two steam-powered cars colliding in Ohio.

In Japan, it's common to have car auctions at temples.

The Volkswagen Beetle was originally designed by Ferdinand Porsche.

In Switzerland, it's illegal to slam a car door too loudly after 10 p.m. to avoid disturbing the peace.

The world's longest traffic jam happened in China in 2010 and lasted for 12 days, stretching over 60 miles.

In Russia, it's a tradition to "jump" a new car by taking it for a spin over a speed bump before hitting the road.

The longest a person has ever hula-hooped continuously was 74 hours and 54 minutes while driving in a car.

In Saudi Arabia, it's against the law for women to drive, although this law has changed since my last update in 2021.

The first car radio was invented by Paul Galvin in 1930 and was called the "Motorola."

The world's most expensive car ever sold at auction is a 1962 Ferrari 250 GTO, which went for $48.4 million.

The Bugatti Veyron can accelerate from 0 to 60 mph in just 2.5 seconds, but it can also drain its fuel tank in just 12 minutes at its top speed of 253 mph.

In some countries, like India and Thailand, it's common to see cars decorated with colorful flowers and ornaments as a form of protection against accidents.

The first recorded instance of road rage occurred in 1907 when a New York City taxi driver got into an argument with a pedestrian.

The iconic DeLorean DMC-12 from the "Back to the Future" movies was originally designed with a brushed stainless steel exterior to avoid the need for paint.

The world's smallest road-legal car is the "Peel P50," which measures just 54 inches long and 41 inches wide.

In Japan, it's not uncommon for drivers to have "washlet" toilet seats in their cars for added comfort during long drives.

The world's largest speeding fine on record was given to a Swedish man who was fined $1 million for driving 180 mph in Switzerland.

In 1924, a Ford Model T car was constructed entirely out of soybeans by Henry Ford as an experiment in sustainable materials.

The first car with a built-in air conditioner was the 1939 Packard, but it was so large it took up most of the trunk space.

The world's first recorded instance of a car being stolen occurred in 1896, just a few years after the first cars were built.

The original name for the Porsche 911 was the "Porsche 901," but it was changed due to a trademark dispute with Peugeot.

In California, it's illegal to whistle for a lost canary while driving your car.

The world's largest car collection is owned by the Sultan of Brunei, who reportedly has over 7,000 cars, including many rare and exotic models.

The "James Bond" franchise has featured many iconic cars, but the most famous is the Aston Martin DB5, which first appeared in "Goldfinger" in 1964.

In 1970s America, custom van culture was so popular that some vans had shag carpeting, waterbeds, and even mini bars inside.

The world's highest mileage car is a 1966 Volvo P1800, which has traveled over 3 million miles with its original owner.

The first car to have seat belts as standard equipment was the 1959 Volvo Amazon.

In Dubai, police officers drive some of the world's fastest and most luxurious cars, including Lamborghinis and Bugattis, as patrol vehicles.

The world's largest car sculpture is the "F1 Race Car" in the United Arab Emirates, which stands at 148 feet tall.

n Russia, it's common for drivers to have dashboard cameras to record their journeys. This practice has captured some incredible and unusual moments on the road.

The "Ice Cream Truck" song, often heard in neighborhoods, was originally a song called "The Whistler and His Dog" and was used to alert children to the arrival of the ice cream vendor.

The "Peugeot 404" was featured in an episode of "The Simpsons" as a car that was virtually indestructible.

In 1941, Henry Ford made a car out of soybeans as an experiment in creating more sustainable vehicles.

In Japan, there's a parking lot with a rooftop garden where you can relax and enjoy the greenery while your car is parked.

The first recorded car accident involving two automobiles happened in New York City in 1896, when cars were still a novelty.

The fastest time to remove a car engine and replace it with a new one is just 42 seconds, achieved by a team of mechanics in 1985.

The original Batmobile from the 1960s TV series was built from a Lincoln Futura concept car and was sold at auction for $4.62 million.

The "Horn Please" sign on trucks in India is not a suggestion but a reminder for other drivers to sound their horns when overtaking.

The "Popemobile" is a specially designed vehicle used by the Pope during public appearances. It often has bulletproof glass and a raised platform to ensure the Pope's safety.

TREES

Some trees, like the quaking aspen, can reproduce by sending up new shoots from their roots, creating "clonal colonies" of genetically identical trees.

The tallest tree in the world, a coast redwood named "Hyperion," stands at a staggering 379.7 feet (115.7 meters) tall.

There's a type of tree called the "Cannonball Tree" that produces large, heavy fruits that can weigh up to 10 pounds and explode upon hitting the ground.

The inner bark of the willow tree contains a natural form of aspirin, which has been used for centuries to relieve pain and reduce fever.

The world's widest tree, the "General Sherman Tree" in California, has a diameter of over 36 feet (11 meters).

The "Pando" tree in Utah is often considered one of the oldest and heaviest living organisms on Earth, estimated to be around 80,000 years old and weighing 6,000 tons.

Some trees can communicate with each other through a network of underground fungal threads called mycorrhizal networks, allowing them to share nutrients and information.

The "Baobab" tree in Africa is known as the "Tree of Life" because it can store thousands of liters of water in its trunk during the dry season.

The "Rainbow Eucalyptus" tree has bark that peels away in strips, revealing a bright green layer underneath, which gradually matures to reveal shades of blue, purple, orange, and maroon.

The "Socotra Dragon Tree" on Socotra Island in Yemen is famous for its umbrella-like canopy and is believed to be up to 6,000 years old.

Trees can "count" the passage of time and adjust their growth rings accordingly. This can be used to study historical climate conditions.

The "Monkey Puzzle" tree, native to Chile, got its unusual name because it was once thought that even monkeys would have a hard time climbing it due to its spiky leaves.

Some trees, like the silver birch, release seeds that are equipped with small wings, allowing them to helicopter down to the ground when they fall.

The scent of pine trees comes from compounds called terpenes, which can have a calming effect and are often used in aromatherapy.

Trees can "move" throughout their lives by growing in the direction of the most available sunlight, a process known as phototropism.

The "Bristlecone Pine" trees in California's White Mountains can live for over 4,000 years, making them some of the oldest living organisms on Earth.

Some trees, like the "Rainforest Tree," can grow up to 100 feet tall without a single branch, with leaves only at the very top to access sunlight.

The "Manchineel Tree" found in the Caribbean is so toxic that standing beneath it during rain can cause skin blistering due to the acidic sap.

In some parts of the world, trees are equipped with mirrors to deter drivers from hitting them and protect both the trees and the vehicles.

The "Whistling Thorn Acacia" tree in Africa has hollow thorns inhabited by ants. When the tree is disturbed, the ants emerge and create a whistling sound by rubbing their bodies against the thorns.

The "Wind Turbine Tree" in Paris is a structure covered with 63 miniature wind turbines that generate clean energy while mimicking the appearance of a tree.

There's a tree in South Africa called the "Sausage Tree" because it produces large, sausage-shaped fruit that can weigh up to 15 pounds each.

The "Octopus Tree" has branches that twist and curl like the tentacles of an octopus, making it look like it came from a fairy tale.

The "Tree of Ténéré" in the Sahara Desert was once considered the most isolated tree on Earth, standing alone for over 250 miles until a drunk driver knocked it down in 1973.

Some trees, like the "Eucalyptus deglupta" or "Rainbow Eucalyptus," shed strips of bark throughout the year, creating a vibrant display of colors on their trunks.

The "Boab Prison Tree" in Australia was used in the 1890s to house prisoners on their way to be tried in the town of Derby.

The "Hydnora africana" is a parasitic plant that grows underground in southern Africa and emerges only to produce foul-smelling, fleshy flowers that attract dung beetles for pollination.

The "Bamboo" is one of the fastest-growing plants in the world and can grow up to 35 inches in a single day under the right conditions.

The "Cherry Tree" that inspired the famous song "Sakura Sakura" in Japan is believed to be over 1,000 years old.

The "Angel Oak Tree" in South Carolina has branches so massive that they have to be propped up to prevent them from touching the ground.

The "Banyan Tree" is known for its aerial roots that grow downward from branches, eventually forming new trunks. These trees can create vast canopies and appear like a small forest on their own.

"Baobab" trees in Africa can store up to 32,000 gallons (120,000 liters) of water in their trunks during the rainy season to survive droughts.

"Cottonwood" trees are named for the cotton-like seeds they produce, which can create "cottonwood blizzards" when they disperse in the wind.

Some trees, like the "Dragon's Blood Tree" found in Socotra, Yemen, exude a red sap that has been used for various purposes, including dye and medicine.

The "Bamboo Lemur" in Madagascar is known to eat bamboo exclusively, making it one of the few primates with such a specialized diet.

The "Angel Oak" in South Carolina, one of the oldest living trees in the United States, is estimated to be between 400 and 500 years old.

The "Rain Tree" is known for its unique habit of folding its leaflets at night, which gives the appearance of drooping leaves when it's dark or raining.

Some trees, like the "Ghost Gum" in Australia, have smooth, pale bark that glows in the moonlight, earning them their eerie name.

The "Methuselah" tree, a bristlecone pine in California, is over 4,800 years old and considered one of the oldest known living organisms on Earth.

The "Monkey Puzzle Tree" is native to South America but is often grown as an ornamental tree in gardens around the world due to its distinctive appearance.

The "Boojum Tree" found in the deserts of Baja California, Mexico, has a tall, slender trunk with branches that resemble upside-down carrots.

"Eucalyptus" trees are known for releasing volatile oils that can create a bluish haze in the air, which can give the Australian landscape a distinctive appearance.